Uncharted, Unexplored, and Unexplained

Scientific Advancements of the 19th Century

Joseph Priestley

and the Discovery of Oxygen

Mitchell Lane
PUBLISHERS

P.O. Box 196
Hockessin, Delaware 19707

Uncharted, Unexplored, and Unexplained

Scientific Advancements of the 19th Century

Titles in the Series

Visit us on the web: www.mitchelllane.com
Comments? email us: mitchelllane@mitchelllane.com

Uncharted, Unexplored, and Unexplained

Scientific Advancements of the 19th Century

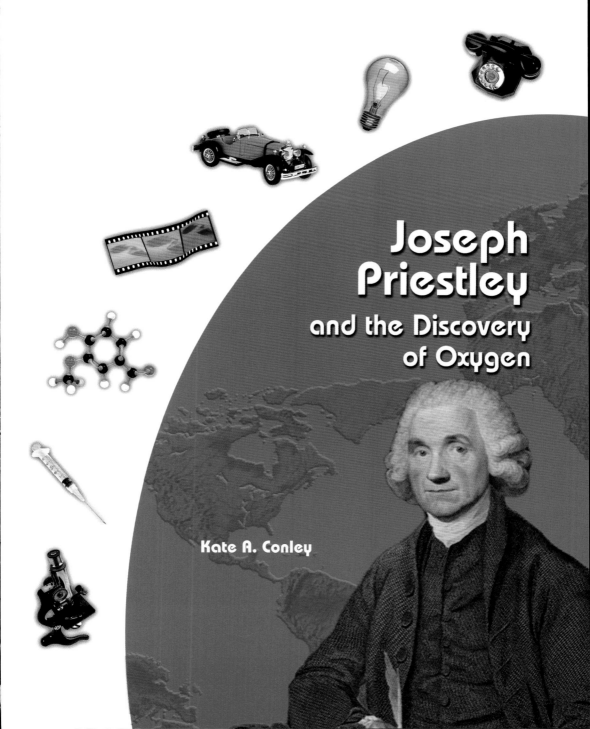

Joseph Priestley

and the Discovery of Oxygen

Kate A. Conley

Uncharted, Unexplored, and Unexplained

Scientific Advancements of the 19th Century

Printing   1   2   3   4   5   6   7   8
    Library of Congress Cataloging-in-Publication Data
Conley, Kate A., 1977–
    Joseph Priestley and the discovery of oxygen / by Kate A. Conley.
        p. cm. — (Uncharted, unexplored, and unexplained)
    Includes bibliographical references and index.
    ISBN 1-58415-367-9 (lib. bdg.)
    1. Priestley, Joseph, 1733–1804—Juvenile literature. 2. Oxygen—Juvenile literature. 3. Chemists—England—Biography—Juvenile literature. 4. Scientists—England—Biography—Juvenile literature. I. Title. II. Series.
QD23.P8C66 2005
540'.92—dc22

                                                                    2004030513

ABOUT THE AUTHOR: Kate A. Conley is a freelance editor and writer. She grew up in suburban Minneapolis and graduated from the University of Minnesota with degrees in English and Spanish. Today, Kate's favorite projects are nonfiction books for students in the lower and middle grades, and she especially enjoys writing biographies and histories. Kate currently lives in Golden Valley, Minnesota, with her husband, Vincent.

PHOTO CREDITS: Cover, pp. 1, 3, 6, 10, 12, 15, 16, 23, 24, 26, 31, 32, 34, 37, 38, 39—SCETI: Edgar Fahs Smith Collection; pp. 18, 41—Library of Congress.

PUBLISHER'S NOTE: This story is based on the author's extensive research, which she believes to be accurate. Documentation of such research is contained on page 47.

The internet sites referenced herein were active as of the publication date. Due to the fleeting nature of some web sites, we cannot guarantee they will all be active when you are reading this book.

Uncharted, Unexplored, and Unexplained

Scientific Advancements of the 19th Century

Joseph Priestley
and the Discovery of Oxygen

*For Your Information

As a young man, Joseph Priestley chose not to enter into the family business of cloth making. Instead, he decided to continue his formal education and become a minister. This path eventually led to prestigious teaching jobs and the opportunity to experiment in science, one of Priestley's lifelong passions.

1

The Boy from Fieldhead

In the 1700s, Fieldhead, England, was a sleepy village. Although it was located just six miles from the bustling city of Leeds, Fieldhead had none of the trappings of a large city. Gray stone cottages dotted its landscape. Residents traveled by horseback on its well-worn country lanes. Sheep grazed contentedly in the valleys, and it was not unusual to see children cut through green, fertile fields on their way to school.

Those fertile fields were what many people in the village relied upon to earn a living. Not everyone in Fieldhead was a farmer, however. In fact, this quiet village was in the heart of a thriving cloth-making district. For generations, people living in Fieldhead had been shearing sheep and spinning the wool into thread. They wove the thread into cloth, dressed it, and sold it in markets. After years of perfecting this process, Fieldhead had become known for its lovely woolen fabrics.

One of Fieldhead's many cloth makers was a man named Jonas. Jonas had a large family. It was expected that his sons would go into the cloth-making trade, just as their father and grandfather had done. However, Jonas may have realized early on that Joseph, his eldest son, was fated for something else. While Jonas was busy weaving and dressing woolen fabric, young Joseph was busy with other tasks that had nothing to do with learning how to make cloth.

Joseph was a boy with a bright mind, an excellent memory, and a tireless curiosity about the world around him. According to his brother Timothy, Joseph conducted the first of what would become a lifetime of experiments at the age of eleven. This first experiment focused on spiders. Joseph wanted to know how long they could live without fresh air. He placed several spiders in a bottle with a tight-fitting lid. Then he monitored them to see how many hours they would survive.

Although the results of the spider experiment are unknown, it had awakened something in young Joseph. Before long, he was conducting experiments with levers. He wanted to determine how much weight they could lift. Then Joseph began learning about astronomy. He spent hours outdoors under the dark night sky observing the stars and planets. The natural world and everything in it had become Joseph's own personal laboratory.

This curiosity stayed with Joseph for his entire life. The results of his experiments impacted the ways in which scientists came to understand everything from respiration and combustion to the composition of the human body and the crust of the Earth. That's because the boy from Fieldhead who had once experimented with spiders grew into the man who discovered the most abundant element on Earth. That man was Joseph Priestley, and the element he discovered was oxygen.

DAILY LIFE IN 18TH-CENTURY ENGLAND

KIRSTIN OLSEN

This book gives a study of England during the 18th century and provides lots of information for students and people interested in reading the everyday details of living life in England in this era.

In many ways, Joseph Priestley's eighteenth-century world was much different than life today. For example, people could not turn on their computer and send an e-mail to a friend. They had to rely on the slow-moving postal service to deliver a handwritten letter. Driving a car to the market or to visit a friend was not an option either. People had to walk, ride horses, or take stagecoaches.

Schools were also much different in that era. Because of religious tensions, many churches founded their own schools. A number of schools charged fees to attend. It was also common for individual teachers to start their own schools. If they moved or fell out of favor with town leaders, the school closed. Schools brimming with bright students one year could easily be gone the next year. As a result, many children did not attend school regularly. Instead, what they learned came from sources such as nursery rhymes, church sermons, their parents, and traveling scholars.

For many children who came from poor families, the chance to even attend school was a luxury. These children had duties that were more important than going to school. Children as young as four or five regularly washed laundry, spun and wove wool, or did farm chores. If a child's family owned a shop, he or she was expected to work in it. In London, many poor children accepted the difficult, dirty, and often dangerous job of working as chimney sweeps.

While most people had to spend long hours working, they were still able to find ways to have a little fun. Since families did not have televisions, movie theaters, or radios, they had to entertain themselves. Many ice-skated in the winter and swam in the summer. They played cards as well as board games such as checkers, chess, and backgammon. Families might stage plays in their homes. Or if they had a little extra money, they could attend a play or concert in a local theater.

Joseph Priestley's early life was rocky, beginning with his mother's death. Then illness, a speech impediment, and a disastrous job filled his life for several years. Eventually, Priestley found happiness and success teaching at Warrington Academy.

2

Preacher and Teacher

On Fieldhead's Owler Lane, the cloth maker Jonas Priestley and his wife, Mary, made their home. Jonas and Mary were hardworking, religious people. On March 13, 1733, they had their first child and named him Joseph. The Priestley family grew quickly after Joseph's birth. Within a few years, Mary had four other small children to look after. To ease her burden, she sent Joseph to live with his grandfather when the little boy was four.

Everything changed in December 1739. Mary died while giving birth to her sixth child. Joseph, now six, left his grandfather's house and returned home. Life was difficult there. Jonas was grieving the loss of his wife, working to support his family, and caring for his young children. Seeing his difficulties, Jonas's sister Sarah Keighley offered a helping hand. She arranged for Joseph to stay with her and her husband, John.

At the age of nine, Joseph made the move to his aunt and uncle's house. The Keighleys were wealthy and lived in a manor home called Old Hall, a few miles from the Priestley home. Although they had been married for many years, the Keighleys had no children of their own. When Joseph moved into Old Hall, Sarah and John treated him as if he were their own son.

On March 13, 1733, Joseph Priestley was born in this home in Fairfield, England.

Shortly after Joseph arrived, John died. Left all alone in Old Hall, Joseph and Sarah quickly fell into a routine. Sarah was a deeply religious woman. Joseph joined her in morning and evening prayers every day. Once a week, Joseph attended a meeting with other young men to discuss spirituality, prayer, and religion. He spent the rest of his time attending school. His curiosity and love for learning made him a natural scholar even at a young age. As his studies progressed, it became clear Joseph was especially good at languages. He excelled at Latin, Greek, and Hebrew.

As Joseph grew, Sarah realized that he was a clever boy. She thought it would be a waste for him to become a cloth maker like his father and grandfather. She believed his bright mind could be put to better use. Sarah wanted Joseph to become a minister. Joseph, who had grown into a deeply religious young man himself, agreed to this path for his future.

Illness cut that plan short. When he was sixteen, Joseph suffered from a deadly lung disease thought to be tuberculosis. The illness weakened him considerably, and he no longer had the strength demanded of a minister. This was certainly a disappointment, but Joseph didn't feel sorry for himself. He decided he would learn a trade. With his gift for languages, Joseph believed he could find work as a translator. He taught himself to speak French, Italian, and German.

Doctors advised Joseph that he needed to move to a warmer climate so his lungs could fully heal. The sunny, mild climate of Portugal seemed like an ideal place. Joseph arranged to move there and work as a translator in the capital city of Lisbon. Just before he was scheduled to leave, the unexpected happened. Joseph made a full recovery.

With his health restored, Joseph began to rethink his future as a translator. During the time that he had been ill and facing death, Joseph's faith had deepened. He had never fully given up on his dream to become a minister. Now that he was recovered, Joseph cancelled his plans for traveling to Lisbon. He enrolled in classes that would help him become a minister.

Joseph began attending Daventry Academy in September 1752. He chose to study divinity, which was a five-year program. The first part of the program focused on languages, as well as mathematics, history, logic, and philosophy. Joseph had already completed advanced studies in these subjects before arriving at Daventry, so he was excused from the first two years of classes. He jumped right into the more advanced courses. Joseph thrived in the atmosphere at Daventry, where students were encouraged to ask difficult questions and challenge established ideas.

When Joseph finished his studies at Daventry in 1755, he received an invitation to work at a chapel in Needham Market. His job would be to assist the chapel's elderly minister, Reverend Meadows. The job paid little and Needham Market was a poor, rundown village. That didn't bother Joseph. He was excited to finally work in the ministry. "I flattered myself that I should be useful and happy in that place,"[1] Joseph wrote of the position in Needham Market.

Despite his enthusiasm, the job at Needham Market was a bad fit for Joseph. His views were much more liberal than those of the aging congregation. Before long, Joseph was looked upon with suspicion and dislike. This wasn't his only difficulty. Joseph's salary was much less than he had been promised, and he was barely able to stay out of debt. Beyond that, a speech impediment that Joseph had suffered from for years began to grow worse. "What contributed greatly to my distress," wrote Joseph, "was the impediment in my speech, which had increased so much, as to make preaching very painful."[2]

Word of Joseph's speech impediment and liberal views spread. It was nearly impossible for him to find a job in another church in the area. He began to explore other ways to earn money. He thought about opening a school. Even with Joseph's Daventry training and gift for languages, no families in Needham Market were willing to enroll their children. They believed Joseph was too radical. He abandoned his plans to teach. Instead, he focused on his faith and began writing about theology.

Meanwhile, friends and family members were working to help Joseph secure a new job as a minister. Through the connections of distant relatives, Joseph was invited to work as a minister at a church in Nantwich. Joseph accepted the position and began preaching there in 1758.

Joseph found the conditions at his new job much better. He got along with members of the church well and enjoyed his work. However, only about sixty people attended the church regularly. With so few people to serve, Joseph had extra time for other work. As he had done in Needham Market, Joseph began thinking about establishing a school.

The people in Nantwich were much more open to having Joseph as a teacher. He opened a school in a traditional half-timber building on Hospital Street. Six days a week, from seven in the morning until four in the afternoon, Joseph taught thirty boys and six girls. His courses covered geography, mathematics, science, Greek, and Latin. Joseph also taught English grammar, a great passion of his. He wrote a textbook for his students called *The Rudiments of English Grammar*.

Joseph's reputation as a talented and qualified teacher began to spread. In 1761, he received an offer to teach at Warrington Academy. He was proud of the school he had founded. He enjoyed teaching there and was earning a good living. However, Warrington was considerably larger than Nantwich. It would offer many new opportunities. Joseph accepted the post.

Warrington was much different than any place Joseph had lived before. Situated along the banks of the Mersey River, the city was a

bustling center of trade and industry. Its residents produced glass, pottery, linen, and sails. A local canal transported ships loaded with passengers and freight. Warrington was also easily connected to other large cities. For example, coaches made the trip from Warrington to London twice a week.

Joseph loved his time at Warrington. He fit into the academy with ease, and he quickly made friends with the other teachers working there. In the classroom, Joseph excelled at teaching languages and literature. He also became involved in the academy's library by overseeing its operation and selecting new books for its collection.

Teaching wasn't the only thing that made Joseph happy while he was at Warrington. In June 1762, Joseph married a young woman named Mary Wilkinson. She was the sister of one of his former students at Nantwich. She was a cheerful and pleasant woman. According to Joseph, their marriage "proved a very suitable and happy connexion."[3]

After their wedding, Mary and Joseph settled into married life. They cared for students who lived as boarders in their home, and they enjoyed going to plays and dances with other teachers at the academy.

Their happiness increased in April 1763, when Joseph and Mary had their first child. They named her Sarah, after Joseph's dear aunt.

While Joseph was happy in his personal life, he had grown indifferent about his career. He was, without question, a talented language teacher. His students loved him and his fellow teachers respected him. However, his interests had expanded into areas beyond language and literature. He had become intensely interested in mathematics and science. These subjects would become the focus of the next phase of Joseph's life.

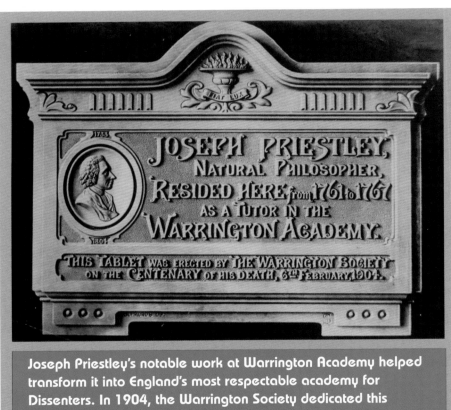

Joseph Priestley's notable work at Warrington Academy helped transform it into England's most respectable academy for Dissenters. In 1904, the Warrington Society dedicated this plaque to Priestley in honor of his accomplishments while at the academy.

During Joseph Priestley's lifetime, religion was an important part of life for nearly everyone living in England. On Sundays most people observed the Sabbath. They went to church services and did not work or travel. People celebrated religious holidays such as Christmas by eating special treats and singing carols. And religious writings, including the Bible and prayer books, were in demand among many families.

The country's official church was the Anglican Church, or the Church of England. It was an incredibly powerful organization. Not only did it oversee the nation's religious faith, it also controlled England's government and many schools. While the majority of the population belonged to the Church of England, there were pockets of people who did not. Joseph Priestley was one of those people.

Joseph and his family members were called Dissenters. Dissenters were a varied group that included Baptists, Lutherans, Methodists, Presbyterians, and Quakers. Though each group held somewhat different beliefs, they all disagreed with the Church of England and had broken away from it.

Cambridge University

Dissenters had limited rights within England. They could vote, but they could not hold a position in the government. They could not attend England's prestigious universities, Oxford and Cambridge. And even though they were not members of the official church, they had to pay a yearly sum of money, known as a tithe, to the Church of England. They did have some freedoms, however. Dissenters could establish their own churches. They could also found their own schools, such as Daventry and Warrington academies.

Despite these limited rights, Joseph embraced his faith. In 1762, while teaching at Warrington Academy, Joseph was ordained as a Dissenting minister. He said, "I bless God that I was born a Dissenter, not manacled by chains of so debasing a system as that of the Church of England, and that I was not educated at Oxford or Cambridge."[4]

The EARL of SHELBURNE.

After a long and successful career at Warrington Academy, Joseph Priestley accepted employment with William Petty, Earl of Shelburne (shown here). Petty was a powerful leader in English government and society, and working for him offered Priestley new opportunities to advance his interests in science.

3

A Budding Scientist

During the late 1700s, students who flocked to the stately red brick building of Warrington Academy received an excellent education. Their courses included divinity, mathematics, science, languages, and literature. Residents of Warrington were quite proud of their academy. They began referring to it as "the Athens of north England."[1] Athens was a city in Greece that had been a center of learning in ancient times.

Finding himself in such a scholarly setting inspired Joseph. He found the academy a wonderful place to nurture his interest in science and mathematics. This interest was not new. It had begun when Joseph was a curious young boy, and it grew as he took science courses at Daventry. Even on school vacations, Joseph was likely to be found reading books such as *Elements of Algebra* and *Dictionary of Arts and Sciences*.

However, Joseph's talent for languages had overshadowed his budding interest in science for many years. That all changed at Warrington Academy. During Joseph's first years of teaching at the academy, he was given great freedom to explore his interests in science. In addition to his Latin, Greek, and literature courses, academy leaders allowed him to teach classes on anatomy. When the academy hosted a series of lectures on chemistry, Joseph eagerly attended them.

This environment rekindled Joseph's curiosity about the natural world. He became interested in conducting his own experiments. No longer would they be the simple experiments of his youth, however. Joseph was ready to tackle a new branch of science: electricity.

Electricity had become a popular topic at this time. It was also what Joseph described as "my own favorite amusement."[2] He would hold experiments on electricity "with a view to amuse myself and my friends."[3] Joseph certainly wasn't the only person conducting experiments on electricity. The leader in the field was an American colonist by the name of Benjamin Franklin.

Franklin had conducted successful experiments with electricity and published his results in several books. Joseph was familiar with these books, as well as Franklin's experiments. He grew terribly excited when he learned that Franklin was traveling from the American colonies to London. At once, Joseph made arrangements to meet Franklin.

In December 1765, Joseph made the difficult three-day journey from Warrington to London. He was a charming man, and upon meeting Franklin the two men quickly became friends. While in London, Joseph also met other notable scientists, including John Canton. Canton was the first man in England to verify Franklin's electricity experiments. Joseph journeyed back to Warrington with a renewed passion.

He began to work on a book about the history of discoveries in electricity. Franklin, Canton, and the other scientists Joseph had met in London were a great help with the project. They helped him find books and scientific equipment for his research. They encouraged him to repeat the experiments of other scientists, as well as conduct his own experiments. They gave him friendly advice and offered feedback on his drafts.

Although Joseph had to give lectures for five hours every day, he spent the rest of his time working on the book. The people who had helped Joseph with the book wanted to make sure his hard work would be well received. So in a letter to Canton, Joseph wrote, "My friends here imagine it would be a great advantage to the publication, if I were a fellow of the Royal Society, and have persuaded me to be a candidate for that honor."[4]

The Royal Society is England's oldest scientific organization. To become a member, Joseph needed other people who belonged to the Society to recommend him. Franklin, Canton, and several other scientists were happy to do so. Joseph became a fellow of the Royal Society in June 1766. The next year, the project into which he had poured all of his energy was finally completed with the publication of *The History and Present State of Electricity*.

Joseph's book was successful among scientists, and critics praised it. However, his success was overshadowed by a growing problem. The supporters of Warrington Academy were slowly withdrawing their funding from the school. The job had never paid much to begin with, and Joseph couldn't afford to stay there much longer. In addition to money problems, Joseph's wife, Mary, was in poor health. Under those conditions, the Priestleys were eager to leave Warrington.

Fortunately, an opportunity quickly presented itself. A few months after his book was published, Joseph received an offer to become a minister at Mill Hill Chapel in Leeds. It would allow Joseph to return to the cloth-making district of his youth, earn a greater living, and try his hand at preaching once again. Mary and Joseph jumped at the opportunity and moved to Leeds in September 1767.

Leeds was growing. New luxuries, such as running water and oil street lamps, were being installed across the city. Leeds had two newspapers, a theater, concert halls, and new turnpikes. The Priestleys enjoyed the busy, urban atmosphere of their new hometown. Their happiness grew shortly after they arrived in Leeds, when Mary gave birth to Joseph Jr. in 1768. Just three years later, the Priestleys had another son, William.

Joseph's young, growing family kept him busy. So did his other responsibilities. He was devoted to his job as minister to the people of Mill Hill Chapel. He preached on Sundays and taught classes in religion to children and adults. Joseph also spent many hours writing articles on government, science, and religion. Beyond that, he helped establish a library in Leeds and oversaw its operation. And he continued to experiment in science.

He acquired new scientific equipment for his research, such as a telescope and a microscope. Joseph also built his own equipment for specific experiments. Although he was still interested in electricity, Joseph began to branch out into other types of science. He studied topics such as optics, light, and color. He also studied gases, the topic that would eventually make him famous.

His first discovery came about because of the location of his house. It was next to a brewery, which gave off a peculiar odor. The odor came from the brewery's vats, where liquid was fermented into ale and beer. As the liquid fermented, it gave off a gas known at the time as "fixed air" (known today as carbon dioxide). Joseph became curious about this fixed air and began to experiment on it.

These experiments involved fire, smoke, and water. When he placed burning pieces of wood into the fixed air, for example, he noticed that the fire rapidly extinguished. In order to see fixed air, which was invisible, Joseph mixed it with smoke. He noticed that the fixed air sank low to the ground. He reasoned that fixed air must be heavier than common air. Joseph also dissolved fixed air into water, which produced bubbles. This bubbly water, known as soda water, was the forerunner of today's soda pop.

To share his findings, Joseph began writing articles and pamphlets about his experiments with fixed air and soda water. According to Joseph, these writings "excited a great degree of attention to the subject."[5] Indeed, scientists in England as well as other parts of Europe were fascinated by his work. In 1773, members of the Royal Society presented Joseph with the Copley Medal for his achievements. It was the Society's highest award.

Fixed air wasn't the only gas that Joseph worked with. Two years before winning the Copley Medal, he began to experiment with a gas

This engraving shows some of the equipment Priestley used in his experiments with gases.

he referred to as common air. He placed a burning candle into a vessel of common air, then sealed the vessel. Within a short period, the candle stopped burning. No matter what Joseph tried, he could not get the candle to burn again. He then placed a mint plant into the same sealed container with the candle. A few days later, he tried burning the candle again. This time, the candle burned easily! Joseph knew the plant must be releasing a gas that allowed the candle to burn.

Exactly what gas the plant had released to allow the candle to burn was a mystery to Joseph. "In what manner the process in nature operates to produce so remarkable an effect I do not pretend to know," he wrote. However, he did know that "vegetation did restore bad air."[6] Without realizing it, Joseph had just performed the first experiment in photosynthesis.

Today, scientists know that photosynthesis occurs when a plant transforms carbon dioxide into oxygen. Oxygen is necessary for burning to take place. When the candle in the vessel without the plant was burning, it used up all of its available oxygen and went out. When the mint plant was added, it restored oxygen to the vessel and allowed the candle to burn again. Although this explanation was still years away, Joseph was fascinated by working with gases and he continued on.

By the time Joseph received the Copley Medal, he had been living in Leeds for six years. He was ready for a change when William Petty, Earl of Shelburne, approached him with a job offer. Petty asked Joseph to become his personal librarian. The job would include a generous salary, a large home, and the freedom to continue preaching and experimenting as Joseph saw fit.

Joseph accepted the job. In May 1773, Mary prepared the family to move to the town of Calne in southern England. According to one account of their move, "Mary packs the bags and Joseph offers to rope them up. She leaves him to it, but when she undoes the truck after the long trip south she finds that under every lid lies a mass of flasks, chemicals, and minerals, tenderly packed in the linen. She is not to worry if the clothes are 'a little injured,' Priestley says, as his equipment has survived the journey beautifully."[7] Joseph's mind was clearly focused on his beloved science, and he was poised to make his biggest discovery yet.

Nearly 150 years after Joseph Priestley received the Copley Medal, the American Chemical Society created its own award in Priestley's honor. The society presents the Priestley Medal to scientists who have made outstanding contributions to the field of chemistry.

Benjamin Franklin

One of the most influential men in Joseph Priestley's early career as a scientist was Benjamin Franklin. Franklin was born in Boston, Massachusetts, on January 17, 1706. At the age of twelve, he became an apprentice to his older brother, who was a printer. Before long, Franklin was a successful printer and publisher in his own right. He is best remembered for writing Poor Richard's Almanack, which contained witty sayings such as "Early to bed early and early to rise makes a man healthy, wealthy, and wise."

Franklin was also brimming over with ideas that would make life easier. His many inventions included bifocal glasses, the lightning rod, daylight saving time, and swimming fins. While living in Philadelphia, Franklin helped organize the city's militia, library, and fire department. He helped found what would become the University of Pennsylvania. And as postmaster, Franklin made improvements that sped up the delivery time of mail.

What primarily endeared Franklin to Joseph Priestley was his work with electricity. Franklin's most famous experiment in this field involved lightning. At the time, most people believed lightning was a mysterious force created by God. Franklin believed it was actually a form of electricity. He set out to prove it during a thunderstorm in 1752.

Franklin and his son William flew a kite with a piece of metal attached to it. The piece of metal was struck by lightning. The electricity from the lightning traveled down the kite string and struck a metal key. When Franklin touched his hand to the key, there was an electrical spark! This demonstrated that Franklin's belief was correct.

While Franklin was an accomplished scientist and inventor, he was also a respected statesman. He was dedicated to the American Revolution, and signed both the Declaration of Independence and the U.S. Constitution. He died on April 17, 1790, at the age of eighty-four. Today, more than two hundred years after his death, Franklin is still honored as one of the brightest minds in American history.

Like Joseph Priestley, Swedish chemist Carl Wilhelm Scheele was interested in learning about the properties of a mysterious gas now known as oxygen. Although Scheele isolated the gas two years before Priestley, delays in publishing his results meant that the credit for discovering oxygen went to Priestley.

4

The Discovery of Oxygen

For the men and women of eighteenth-century England, social class determined their fate in life. People such as field hands, miners, peddlers, soldiers, and seamstresses made up the lower class. They worked terribly hard just to scrape by. People who had some education, like ministers, lawyers, and engineers, formed the middle class. They lived in relative comfort. Aristocrats such as dukes, earls, and barons made up the upper class. Aristocrats enjoyed easy lives. They were wealthy property owners who employed servants, traveled across Europe for pleasure, and ruled England.

England's class system was rigid. Opportunities to move up from one class to another were quite rare. Joseph Priestley knew he had one of those rare opportunities in working for William Petty. As a minister, Joseph was squarely in the middle class. Petty was a member of the aristocracy. While working for Petty, Joseph knew he would have access to new and powerful people and resources that would otherwise not have been available to him.

With that in mind, Joseph happily settled into his new job. He arranged Petty's books, indexed his personal papers, and cataloged his entire collection of books and manuscripts. In addition to his duties as librarian, Joseph also served as the resident scholar. He tutored Petty's sons. And he acted as a companion to Petty, who enjoyed talking about literature and other scholarly topics.

Though Joseph's duties to Petty kept him busy, they did not take up all of his time. He still found plenty of hours to spend in his laboratory. In the summer of 1774, Joseph's attention was focused on his newest piece of laboratory equipment: a burning glass. It was a twelve-inch lens that could be used to concentrate the sun's rays, producing an intense heat.

The lens inspired Joseph to perform new experiments. He placed metals into glass containers. Then he set the containers into a basin filled with mercury. Using the lens, Joseph heated the metals. When they were heated, the metals gave off gases that were captured in the glass containers. Joseph studied these captured gases. He placed candles in the containers to see if they burned well in the gas. Or he placed small animals, such as mice, into them to see if the gas supported life.

After repeated experiments, Joseph found that the heat from the lens caused some of the mercury in the basin to turn into a reddish-colored ash. Scientists called it red mercuric oxide. Joseph became curious about what would happen if he heated it. So on August 1, 1774, he set up another experiment just like the others. He heated the ash with the lens until it gave off a gas. He collected the gas in a glass container, then began his routine experiments.

Joseph noticed one striking property of the gas right away. "What surprised me more than I can express," wrote Joseph of this gas, "was that a candle burned in this air with a remarkably vigorous flame."[1] This was a particularly startling revelation. For years, scientists had wondered what chemical process took place during combustion. This gas seemed to offer some kind of clue to that mystery.

Most scientists of this period, including Joseph, mistakenly believed in a popular theory about what happened during combustion. They thought any material capable of burning, such as wood, was rich in a substance called phlogiston (pronounced floe-JIS-tun). When these materials were set on fire, scientists believed that they released phlogiston into the air. When the air could no longer absorb any more phlogiston, the flame died down and finally extinguished itself.

With this theory in mind, Joseph began thinking about his experiment with the gas and the candle. Clearly, he reasoned, the gas could easily absorb all the of the candle's phlogiston, allowing the flame to burn intensely. But why was this happening? Joseph believed it must be because the gas lacked any phlogiston of its own. As a result, it could readily absorb all of the phlogiston that the candle released. For this reason, Joseph named the gas "dephlogisticated air." Joseph published his findings on dephlogisticated air later that year.

Joseph was not the first person to discover this gas. About two years earlier, Swedish chemist Carl Wilhelm Scheele had performed similar experiments. Like Joseph, Scheele had discovered a gas in which flames burned brighter. Scheele named the gas "fire air." Publishing delays meant Scheele had to wait five years before sharing his findings with the public. Joseph, on the other hand, had published his findings almost immediately. As a result, Joseph was credited with discovering the gas.

Pleased with his new discovery, Joseph took a break from the laboratory. Petty asked Joseph to join him on a tour of Europe. Joseph jumped at this benefit of working for a wealthy aristocrat. In October 1774, the two men set off on their journey. They traveled through Belgium, Holland, Germany, and France.

While in France, Joseph and Petty spent time in Paris. There, Joseph had dinner with some of Paris's leading scientists, including Antoine-Laurent Lavoisier. Over the course of the dinner, Joseph explained his discovery of dephlogisticated air. Lavoisier had also been studying gases and was fascinated by Joseph's findings. He immediately began to repeat Joseph's experiments.

In the meantime, Joseph and Petty returned to England. Joseph continued testing dephlogisticated air. His next experiments centered on living creatures. During this era, scientists believed that flaming materials were not the only substances to give off phlogiston. They believed that living creatures released it when they exhaled. When a creature had saturated the air with phlogiston, it would die. Knowing that flames burned brighter in dephlogisticated air, Joseph wondered if an animal could live longer in its presence as well.

Joseph decided to test this theory. In March 1775, he put a mouse into a glass container filled with dephlogisticated air. "Had it been common air," wrote Joseph, "a full-grown mouse, as this was, would have lived in it about a quarter of an hour. In this air, however, my mouse lived a full half-hour."[2]

Though the mouse appeared to be dead, it had only suffered a severe chill. It soon revived. Realizing that the mouse had not been harmed by the experiment, Joseph wanted to see what effect the gas would have on humans. "My reader will not wonder that, after having ascertained the superior goodness of dephlogisticated air by mice living in it . . . I should have the curiosity to taste it myself. I have gratified that curiosity by breathing it . . . The feeling of it to my lungs is not sensibly different of that from common air, but I fancied that my breath felt peculiarly light and easy for some time afterwards,"[3] he commented.

Joseph wasn't the only scientist to experiment with dephlogisticated air. Back in Paris, Lavoisier also experimented with the gas from 1775 to 1780. His work with the gas was brilliant. He was the first person to recognize that the gas was an element and realize that it made up 20 percent of Earth's air. Lavoisier also gave dephlogisticated air its current name: oxygen.

Although Lavoisier was excited about his work with oxygen, he had sharp disagreements with the man who had discovered it. Priestley clung to the mistaken theory of phlogiston. Lavoisier, on the other hand, did not believe this theory could possibly be true. Instead, Lavoisier correctly believed that a substance capable of burning, such as wood or charcoal, must combine with oxygen in the air for combustion to take place. If a fire does not receive oxygen or if the burning substance is completely consumed, the fire dies out.

Joseph Priestley spent many hours in his laboratory while studying oxygen and other gases. This engraving shows the setup of his laboratory, as well as much of the equipment he used in his experiments.

While studying oxygen's role in combustion, Lavoisier began to also wonder about its role in respiration. To test out his ideas, he performed several experiments. From these, he realized that although air was a mixture of different gases, oxygen was the only one of those gases used in respiration. He also realized that the oxygen humans and animals inhale is transformed into a different gas (carbon dioxide) when they exhale.

Just as Lavoisier had built on Joseph's discovery of dephlogisticated air, other scientists continued to build upon Lavoisier's ideas. Modern scientists now know that oxygen is the most abundant element on Earth.

It makes up nearly 90 percent of water, 50 percent of Earth's crust, and 65 percent of the human body. Nearly every living creature, from fish to human beings, needs oxygen to survive.

However, these discoveries were still years away. In the meantime, Joseph was at home in Calne working as Petty's librarian and spending time in his laboratory. He also found time to write a number of articles on government and religion. As had been the case throughout Joseph's career, these writings were highly controversial. Many people criticized Joseph and some even accused him of not believing in God. Others distrusted him because he supported the American colonies rather than England when they declared their independence.

This was upsetting not only for Joseph but also for Petty. The controversial writings had begun to strain their friendship. In 1780, Joseph left his job with Petty. The Priestley family, which now included a new son named Henry, moved to central England. They settled in Birmingham, a large industrial town where Joseph would once again work as a minister. For Joseph, this move would bring great joy as well as deep sorrow.

Joseph Priestley used the equipment pictured here when he isolated oxygen. As the sun's rays passed though the twelve-inch lens, they heated metals that Priestley had placed in the glass vessels. Priestley heated each metal individually, placing its vessel over the basin, which was filled with mercury. By heating the mercury itself, Priestley was finally able to isolate oxygen.

Antoine-Laurent Lavoisier

Antoine-Laurent Lavoisier was born in Paris, France, on August 26, 1743. His mother came from a wealthy family and his father was a respected lawyer. When Lavoisier's mother died when he was just five years old, he was sent to live with an aunt, Constance Punctis. Lavoisier's aunt doted on him, and the two got along well.

At the age of eleven, Lavoisier began attending a school known as Collège Mazarin. Its graduates were some of France's brightest mathematicians and scientists. Lavoisier spent several years at Collège Mazarin and excelled in his courses. Then, following in his father's footsteps, Lavoisier became a lawyer.

By that time, Lavoisier had begun dabbling in science as a hobby. In a short time it became clear that science, not law, was his true passion. One of Lavoisier's friends, a geologist named Jean-Étienne Guettard, helped him explore this passion further. According to Guettard, Lavoisier had "a natural taste for the sciences [that] leads him to want to know all of them before concentrating on one rather than another."[4]

Lavoisier did, in fact, explore several branches of science, from botany to geology. However, chemistry was the one that truly captured his attention. During the course of his career, he became famous for his groundbreaking discoveries surrounding oxygen and its role in combustion and respiration. He is also remembered for the work he did to advance chemistry as a branch of science. In 1787, Lavoisier collaborated with three other scientists to publish a book that created a nomenclature for chemistry, much of which is still in use today. His book Elementary Treatise on Chemistry, *published two years later, provided specific methods that chemists should follow when performing experiments and investigations.*

In the midst of the French Revolution, Lavoisier was accused of loyalty to the royal government. For this reason, he was executed in May 1794. Today, he is recognized as the Father of Modern Chemistry.

33

Although Joseph Priestley had gained fame for his discovery of oxygen, he faced a number of problems in his personal life. His radical beliefs on religion and government earned him the reputation of a troublemaker, and he was eventually forced to flee England for the United States in 1794.

5

From Birmingham to Northumberland

"I highly consider my settlement in Birmingham the happiest event in my life,"[1] wrote Joseph in his memoir. Indeed, life did seem to be good for the Priestleys as they settled in Birmingham. Joseph's brother-in-law found them a large, beautiful home called Fair Hill. Joseph quickly built a laboratory and it became a great joy for him. Not only was it a place of research and discovery, but it also became a place of laughter and fun.

Now that Joseph's children had grown older, he encouraged them and their friends to join him in the laboratory and play there. One of their favorite "toys" was an old air gun. They made a game out of setting up Joseph's wig block as a target and then aiming at it with the air gun. Though games like this were noisy and disruptive, Joseph enjoyed having the children around, even when he was working.

Added to this joy was Joseph's return to the ministry. The chapel at which he preached, the New Meeting House, was one of the largest, wealthiest, and most liberal Dissenting churches in England. He was a popular preacher, and the congregation grew. Catherine Hutton, one of the people who regularly attended services at the New Meeting House, said, "In the pulpit he is mild, persuasive and unaffected, as his sermons are full of good reasoning and sound sense. He is not what is called an orator; he uses no action, no declamation; but his voice and manner are those of one friend speaking to another."[2]

In addition to preaching, Joseph had other duties such as organizing Sunday school classes and tending to the needs of his church members. As he had done in Leeds, Joseph became involved in Birmingham's library, which had started just a year before he arrived. It was a small collection of books stored in a closet. Once Joseph became involved, he moved the library from the closet to a proper room, arranged for the purchase of new books, hired a librarian, and established rules for using the library.

Amid this work, Joseph also found time to become involved in Birmingham's scientific club, the Lunar Society. Its name came because meetings were held on nights of the full moon, which provided enough light so the members could find their way home in safety. They included some of the most influential and original thinkers in science and industry during this period: Matthew Boulton (creator of one of the world's first modern factories), James Watt (inventor of the first steam engine with practical uses), and Josiah Wedgwood (innovator in the field of industrial pottery). These men provided a support network for Joseph while he continued to conduct scientific research.

During this period, Joseph found himself increasingly at odds with England's government and church. Some of the religious books he had written were quite radical, and leaders of the Church of England became leery of him. England's leaders viewed him as a troublemaker for his political views. He supported reforming England's Parliament. He also became an outspoken supporter of the French Revolution, which encouraged democracy rather than rule by a king and aristocrats. England's king and aristocrats worried that the same thing could happen in their own country. They wanted to squash any support for the French Revolution.

Tensions grew steadily and erupted into violence on July 14, 1791. That evening, an angry group of people who supported the Church of England and the English government, referred to as the "Church-and-King" mob, singled out Joseph. The mob's first stop was the New

Like Priestley, James Watt was a member of the Lunar Society. Watt was famous for his improvements to the steam engine, which made it more practical to operate. Watt's improved steam engines became widely used in mills across England, contributing to the growth of modern industry.

Meeting House. They ripped out the pews, destroyed the church library, and finally set fire to the building.

Mary and Joseph were at home at Fair Hill playing a game of backgammon. One of their friends, Samuel Ryland, burst in and warned them that the mob was coming. The Priestleys fled to the home of a nearby friend for safety.

Shortly afterward, the mob descended on Fair Hill. They broke down the doors and began destroying everything inside. Outside, they toppled trees and shrubs. Then they turned to the laboratory and began smashing Joseph's scientific equipment. As a final blow, they set the house and laboratory on fire.

It was a clear, bright night. Joseph witnessed the attack firsthand from the safety of his friend's home. "We could see a considerable distance, and being upon rising ground we distinctly heard all that passed at the house, every shout of the mob, and almost every stroke of the instruments that have provided for breaking the doors and furniture,"[3] he wrote.

By dawn, the riots had ended. Joseph's home and church were in ruins. If that wasn't bad enough, he received word that rioters were preparing to gather again. This time Joseph himself was the target. His life was in danger. Joseph promptly left Birmingham and traveled to a friend's home in London. While he was in the relative safety of London, the mob continued to destroy the property of Birmingham's Dissenters.

Joseph Priestley's outspokenness about England's government and his liberal religious views made him an easy target of violence. On the night of July 14, 1791, Priestley and his wife watched helplessly as rioters destroyed their home in Birmingham.

When the riots finally ended, four churches and twenty-seven homes had been destroyed.

Joseph knew he could not return to Birmingham. Instead, he and his wife attempted to start over in Hackney, near London. Joseph continued writing and also spent time teaching, serving as a minister, and rebuilding his laboratory. However, many people, including members of the Royal Society, shunned Joseph for his radical viewpoints. "My own situation, if not hazardous, [had] become unpleasant, so that I thought my removal would be of more service to the cause of truth than my longer stay in England,"[4] wrote Joseph years later.

With that, Joseph and Mary packed their belongings and prepared for yet another move. This time they would be traveling much farther than ever before. Instead of a taking a coach ride across England, they boarded a ship that would take them to the United States.

The Priestleys left England on April 8, 1794. After an eight-week journey, they landed in New York. Unlike their situation in England, the Priestleys were greeted with respect and warmth in the United States. Although they were invited to live in New York and Philadelphia, the Priestleys declined those offers. They had another community in mind.

Joseph and Mary chose to settle in Northumberland, Pennsylvania. It was a community originally intended as a haven for English citizens fleeing political persecution. As such, it seemed like the perfect fit for the Priestleys. The community held an even stronger attraction. All three

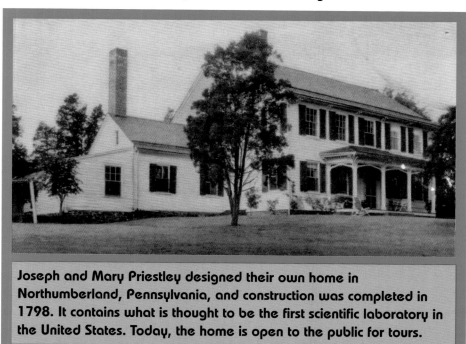

Joseph and Mary Priestley designed their own home in Northumberland, Pennsylvania, and construction was completed in 1798. It contains what is thought to be the first scientific laboratory in the United States. Today, the home is open to the public for tours.

of their sons settled there when they had immigrated to the United States years earlier.

Upon arriving in Northumberland, the Priestleys lived with Joseph Jr., his wife Elizabeth, and their children. Soon Joseph and Mary began designing a new home of their own. It would be a grand, federal-style house. As construction began, it seemed that everything was finally going peacefully. However, that peace was shattered a short time later. Priestley's favorite son, Henry, died in December 1795. Mary died of tuberculosis the following September.

Saddened but unwilling to give up, Joseph returned to his three passions: science, religion, and politics. He created a laboratory and continued his experiments with gases. One result was the discovery of carbon monoxide. He also wrote about religion, preached, and helped found First Unitarian Church in Philadelphia. In the world of politics, Joseph found the going hard. Some Americans were leery of his support for France, which by now had become an enemy of the United States after providing crucial support during the American Revolution. Others disliked his decidedly English religious beliefs. Joseph's alleged criticism of the U.S. government led the secretary of state, Timothy Pickering, to ask for Joseph to be deported.

Despite Pickering's request, Joseph was allowed to stay in the United States. The situation improved when Joseph's powerful friend, Thomas Jefferson, became president in 1801. Jefferson asked Joseph's opinion on education reforms and complimented his religious writings. According to Joseph, "I now, for the first time in my life (and I shall soon enter my seventieth year), find myself in any degree of favor with the government of the country in which I have lived, and I hope I shall die in the same pleasing situation."[5]

On February 6, 1804, a little more than a year after writing those words, Joseph Priestley died. Today, scholars are continuing to unravel the life of this complex, innovative thinker. One biographer described the challenges of studying Joseph's life by saying that he was "equally at home in the laboratory, investigating electricity and discovering gases, as he was in the church, puzzling out the mysteries of the Book of

Timothy Pickering led the charge for Joseph Priestley to be deported from the United States. Pickering was a powerful leader who had served as a general in the Continental Army and a representative at the Constitutional Convention. Despite Pickering's influence in government, Priestley was allowed to remain in the United States.

Revelation."[6] Added to that complexity is the fact that most of Joseph's letters and other personal papers were destroyed by Birmingham riots. As a result, most of what scholars know of Joseph's life comes from his published works, letters that his friends received from him, and a short memoir he wrote near the end of his life.

Although the man remains somewhat of a mystery, his discovery of oxygen plays a clear role in modern science. For example, people suffering from carbon monoxide poisoning, burns, or smoke inhalation are often placed in special chambers where they breathe pure oxygen to aid recovery. Oxygen is highly flammable, so it is a powerful fuel for rockets. Airplane pilots and mountain climbers use oxygen when traveling in high altitudes. Scuba divers are able to stay underwater for long periods thanks to the oxygen tanks they carry. With these and many other uses, Joseph's eighteenth-century discovery lives on in the twenty-first century world.

The Fall of Bastille

The French Revolution began in 1789. However, the events leading to it had begun much earlier. For years, French society had been divided into three parts: the First Estate (clergy), the Second Estate (nobles), and the Third Estate (commoners). The First and Second Estates controlled the nation, while the Third Estate was nearly powerless and had grown angry. Adding to the unrest were poor harvests, a group of influential French writers who promoted reform, and a government that was nearly broke.

To solve the government's money problems, King Louis XVI called a meeting of all three Estates in May 1789. At the meeting, representatives of the Third Estate demanded reforms. They wanted all the Estates to join into one assembly in which each representative had one vote. They also wanted to create a constitution. These were early steps toward establishing a democracy in France.

The king and other Estates refused to accept the reforms. Representatives of the Third Estate left the meeting in June. They declared themselves the National Assembly of France and planned to write a constitution. Eventually, King Louis XVI allowed the three Estates to join in one assembly. But the damage had been done. The king distrusted the Third Estate and began gathering troops. The revolution was underway.

One of the revolution's most notable events took place on July 14, 1789, when French commoners seized the Bastille. This massive stone fortress in Paris housed weapons that the commoners believed they could use to defend themselves against the king's troops. The Bastille was more than just a place to store weapons. It also represented the oppressive French government. Its capture was a symbol of hope and triumph.

The storming of the Bastille was the beginning of the French Revolution, which lasted another ten years. During that time, thousands of people suffered and died to defend their freedoms. This noble spirit captured the imagination of Joseph Priestley. His support for the French Revolution, along with other radical views, made him the target of hatred and violence.

42

Chronology

1733	Born in Fieldhead, England, on March 13
1739	Mother dies
1742	Moves in with aunt and uncle, Sarah and John Keighley
1749	Contracts tuberculosis but recovers
1752	Begins attending Daventry Academy to become a minister
1755	Takes first job as a minister at Needham Market
1758	Moves to Nantwich to preach and begin a school
1761	Begins teaching at Warrington Academy
1762	Marries Mary Wilkinson
1765	Travels to London to meet Benjamin Franklin and other leading scientists
1766	Becomes a member of the Royal Society
1767	Publishes *The History and Present State of Electricity*; moves to Leeds, where he works as a preacher and experiments with photosynthesis and carbon dioxide
1773	Receives Copley Medal from the Royal Society for his work with carbon dioxide; moves to Calne to work for William Petty, Earl of Shelburne
1774	Discovers oxygen; travels in Europe and meets French chemist Antoine-Laurent Lavoisier
1780	Moves to Birmingham to work as a minister
1791	Loses church and home to a mob that is angry about his outspoken views; tries unsuccessfully to resettle near London
1794	Immigrates to the United States
1799	Discovers carbon monoxide
1804	Dies at Northumberland, Pennsylvania, on February 6

Timeline of Discovery

1500   Italian painter and scientist Leonardo da Vinci is the first European to suggest that air is not a single element but rather a combination of two gases.

1669   English scientist John Mayow studies what he calls *spiritus nitroaereus* (oxygen).

1697   German physician Georg Ernest Stahl proposes the phlogiston theory.

1754   English scientist Joseph Black discovers "fixed air" (carbon dioxide).

1766   English scientist Henry Cavendish discovers hydrogen.

1772   Swedish scientist Carl Wilhelm Scheele discovers fire-air (oxygen), but delays publishing his results for five years.

1774   Joseph Priestley is credited with discovering oxygen.

1775   French scientist Antoine-Laurent Lavoisier begins conducting experiments on dephlogisticated air, correctly recognizing it as an element and understanding its role in respiration and combustion.

1789   Lavoisier changes the name of dephlogisticated air to oxygen.

1798   Thomas Beddoes opens the Pneumatic Institute in England, making it the first clinic to employ widespread use of oxygen in medical care.

1805   French scientist Joseph Louis Gay-Lussac proves that water is a combination of one part oxygen and two parts hydrogen.

1839   Welch scientist William Robert Grove invents the fuel cell by combining oxygen with hydrogen to produce electrical power.

1926   Physics professor Robert Goddard successfully launches the first rocket fueled by liquid oxygen.

1943   Frenchmen Jacques Cousteau and Émile Gagnan invent the Aqua-Lung, the first compressed-air system to provide oxygen to divers while underwater.

1987   Scientists interested in the study of oxygen form the Oxygen Society.

1997   America's first oxygen bar opens in Los Angeles, California, allowing patrons to smell scented oxygen.

2004   Energy companies experiment with fuel additives that contain oxygen activators, which allow fuel to burn more efficiently and reduce pollution.

2005   The American Lung Association praises the FAA for issuing a long overdue rule to make commercial air travel easier for patients who rely on oxygen. The rule will allow airlines to permit patients to travel with portable oxygen concentrators during all phases of the flight.

Chapter Notes

Chapter 2   Preacher and Teacher

1. Joseph Priestley, *Autobiography of Joseph Priestley* (London: Adams & Dart, 1970), p. 78.

2. Ibid., p. 80.

3. Ibid., p. 87.

4. Jenny Uglow, *The Lunar Men: Five Friends Whose Curiosity Changed the World* (New York: Farrar, Straus, and Giroux, 2002), p. 71.

Chapter 3   A Budding Scientist

1. Robert E. Schofield, *The Enlightenment of Joseph Priestley: A Study of His Life and Work from 1733 to 1773* (University Park, PA: The Pennsylvania State University Press, 1997), p. 88.

2. Ibid., p. 139.

3. Ibid., p. 139.

4. Ibid., p. 143.

5. Joseph Priestley, *Autobiography of Joseph Priestley* (London: Adams & Dart, 1970), p. 95.

6. Robert E. Schofield, *The Enlightenment of Joseph Priestley: A Study of His Life and Work from 1733 to 1773* (University Park, PA: The Pennsylvania State University Press, 1997), p. 266.

7. Jenny Uglow, *The Lunar Men: Five Friends Whose Curiosity Changed the World* (New York: Farrar, Straus, and Giroux, 2002), p. 225.

Chapter 4   The Discovery of Oxygen

1. Jenny Uglow, *The Lunar Men: Five Friends Whose Curiosity Changed the World* (New York: Farrar, Straus, and Giroux, 2002), p. 229.

2. Ibid., p. 230.

3. I. Bernard Cohen, *Album of Science: From Leonardo to Lavoisier, 1450–1800* (New York: Charles Scribner's Sons, 1980), pp. 139–40.

4. Charles Coulston Gillispie, *Dictionary of Scientific Biography*, Volume viii (New York: Charles Scribner's Sons, 1973), p. 68.

Chapter 5   From Birmingham to Northumberland

1. Joseph Priestley, *Autobiography of Joseph Priestley* (London: Adams & Dart, 1970), p. 120.

2. Jenny Uglow, *The Lunar Men: Five Friends Whose Curiosity Changed the World* (New York: Farrar, Straus, and Giroux, 2002), p. 406.

3. Ibid., p. 442.

4. Joseph Priestley, *Autobiography of Joseph Priestley* (London: Adams & Dart, 1970), p. 132.

5. Ibid., p. 32.

6. Leslie Alan Horvitz, *Eureka! Scientific Breakthroughs That Changed the World* (New York: John Wiley & Sons, 2002), p. 22.

Glossary

aristocrat (uh-RISS-tuh-krat)—a member of the aristocracy, a social class having wealth and power.

combustion (cum-BUS-chun)—the process of burning.

congregation (kahng-gruh-GAY-shun)—a group of people who meet to worship together.

deport (dee-PORT)—force a person to leave a country.

divinity (duh-VIH-nuh-tee)—a divine being, such as God.

dress (DRESS)—put a product, such as cloth, through a finishing process before sending it to market.

element (EH-leh-ment)—one of more than one hundred basic chemical substances; oxygen, carbon, lead, and sodium are examples of elements.

ferment (fur-MENT)—to undergo the process by which sugar in a liquid is converted to alcohol and carbon dioxide.

memoir (MEM-war)—the story of a person's life as written by that person.

nomenclature (NO-mun-klay-chur)—the terms used in a certain field, such as science or art.

optics (AWP-ticks)—the branch of science that studies light and its properties.

respiration (res-puh-RAY-shun)—the process of breathing.

saturate (SAH-chuh-rate)—to fill to capacity.

speech impediment (SPEECH im-PEH-duh-munt)—a difficulty, such as stuttering or lisping, that prevents a person from speaking clearly and smoothly.

theology (thee-AW-luh-gee)—the study of religion.

For Further Reading

For Young Adults

Blashfield, Jean F. *Oxygen*. Austin, TX: Raintree Steck-Vaughn, 1998.

Farndon, John. *Oxygen*. New York: Benchmark Books, 1999.

Kjelle, Marylou Morano. *Antoine Lavoisier: Father of Modern Chemistry*. Newark, DE: Mitchell Lane Publishers, 2005.

Works Consulted

Cohen, I. Bernard. *Album of Science: From Leonardo to Lavoisier, 1450–1800*. New York: Charles Scribner's Sons, 1980.

Gillispie, Charles Coulston. *Dictionary of Scientific Biography*. Volume viii. New York: Charles Scribner's Sons, 1973.

———. *Dictionary of Scientific Biography*. Volume xi. New York: Charles Scribner's Sons, 1975.

Horvitz, Leslie Alan. *Eureka! Scientific Breakthroughs That Changed the World*. New York: John Wiley & Sons, 2002.

Olsen, Kirstin. *Daily Life in 18th-Century England*. Westport, CT: Greenwood Press, 1999.

Priestley, Joseph. *Autobiography of Joseph Priestley*. London: Adams & Dart, 1970.

Schofield, Robert E. *The Enlightenment of Joseph Priestley: A Study of His Life and Work from 1733 to 1773*. University Park, PA: The Pennsylvania State University Press, 1997.

Silverman, Sharon Hernes. "Joseph Priestley: Catalyst of the Enlightenment," *Pennsylvania Heritage Magazine*, volume xxv, number 3, summer 1999.

Uglow, Jenny. *The Lunar Men: Five Friends Whose Curiosity Changed the World*. New York: Farrar, Straus, and Giroux, 2002.

On the Internet

Benjamin Franklin
http://www.pbs.org/benfranklin/

Chemical Achievers: Joseph Priestley
http://www.chemheritage.org/EducationalServices/chemach/fore/jp.html

Joseph Priestley: Discoverer of Oxygen
http://center.acs.org/landmarks/landmarks/priestley/index.html

The Lunar Society
http://www.lunarsociety.org.uk/

The Royal Society
http://www.royalsoc.ac.uk/

The Story of Joseph Priestley
http://www.phmc.state.pa.us/bah/priestly/

Index